Food Dudes

JOHN PEMBERTON:

Coca-Cola Developer

Sheila Griffin Llanas

**Checkerboard
Library**

An Imprint of Abdo Publishing
www.abdopublishing.com

www.abdopublishing.com

Published by Abdo Publishing, a division of ABDO, PO Box 398166, Minneapolis, Minnesota 55439. Copyright © 2015 by Abdo Consulting Group, Inc. International copyrights reserved in all countries. No part of this book may be reproduced in any form without written permission from the publisher. Checkerboard Library™ is a trademark and logo of Abdo Publishing.

Printed in the United States of America, North Mankato, Minnesota.
052014
092014

 **THIS BOOK CONTAINS RECYCLED MATERIALS**

Cover Photos: Corbis, Getty Images
Interior Photos: Alamy pp. 8, 12; AP Images pp. 10, 19, 20, 23, 25, 27; Corbis pp. 1, 5, 9, 13; iStockphoto pp. 11, 17, 21, 22; Library of Congress pp. 7, 15, 16; Wikimedia Commons p. 7

Series Coordinator: Megan M. Gunderson
Editor: Heidi M.D. Elston
Art Direction: Neil Klinepier

Library of Congress Cataloging-in-Publication Data

Llanas, Sheila Griffin, 1958-
 John Pemberton : Coca-Cola developer / Sheila Griffin Llanas.
     pages cm. -- (Food dudes)
  ISBN 978-1-62403-317-9
 1. Pemberton, John, 1831-1888--Juvenile literature. 2. Coca-Cola Company--History--Juvenile literature. 3. Soft drink industry--United States--History--Juvenile literature. 4. Businessmen--United States--Biography. I. Title.
  HD9349.S632P456 2015
  338.7'66362092--dc23
  [B]
                                            2014000103

Contents

Georgia Childhood

Today, Coca-Cola is a world-famous soda. More than 100 years ago, a **pharmacist** named Doc Pemberton invented the recipe as a medicine. But Coca-Cola tasted too good to be sipped just for headaches. As more people tasted it, Doc's medicine became a popular soft drink.

John Stith Pemberton was born on January 8, 1831. His parents were Martha and James Clifford Pemberton. The family lived in Knoxville, which is in central Georgia. It was a small town, but it sat on a **stagecoach** route between Washington, DC, and New Orleans, Louisiana. Soon, the Pembertons moved to Rome, in northwestern Georgia.

John grew up in a time when the United States was still new. In his home state, settlers traveled on horseback, in wagons, or by stagecoach. Soon, steamboats and trains made stops in John's town. He saw the country change. Industrial growth led to many new inventions. His famous soda would be one of them!

When John Pemberton died, he was praised as "a popular gentleman" and "the oldest druggist of Atlanta and one of her best known citizens."

Family & Career

Pemberton did not plan to be a food inventor. He hoped to be a doctor. He graduated from the Reform Medical College of Georgia in Macon in 1850. He earned a license to practice medicine at just 19 years old. For a time, he worked as a surgeon. But his true interest was medical **chemistry**. So, he later earned a graduate degree in **pharmacy** in Philadelphia, Pennsylvania.

In 1853, Pemberton married Ann Eliza Clifford "Cliff" Lewis of Columbus, Georgia. The couple's only son, Charles Ney, was born the next year. They bought a house in Columbus on November 20, 1855, for $1,950.

In 1855, Pemberton founded a wholesale and retail drug business. He sold the ingredients that were used to make medicines. In Pemberton's era, many medicines were based on herbal home remedies.

Unfortunately, like many others, Pemberton's career and family life were interrupted when the **Civil War** began in 1861. Pemberton **enlisted** in May 1862 and served as a lieutenant colonel in the

CONFEDERATES SET FIRE TO LOWER BRIDGE

Early in the afternoon of April 16, 1865, the first major act in the Battle of Girard-Columbus took place. Union General Emory Upton sent the First Ohio cavalry charging down old Crawford Road to capture the Dillingham Bridge, then known as the lower or wagon bridge. Confederates on the Georgia side had prepared for the Union tactic by removing the bridge's flooring and placing turpentine-soaked cotton along the length of its superstructure. Confederate Colonel C. C. McGehee crawled out on the wooden framework and set it ablaze. When they saw the bridge burst into flame, the First Ohio broke off its all-out charge.

ERECTED BY THE HISTORIC CHATTAHOOCHEE COMMISSION AND THE PHENIX CITY-RUSSELL COUNTY CHAMBER OF COMMERCE 2004

Bridges crossing the Chattahoochee River were key parts of the Battle of Columbus. The town was important because it produced supplies for the war.

Many consider the Battle of Columbus the last major battle of the Civil War.

Confederate army. He organized the Third Georgia Cavalry Battalion to help defend his town.

At the end of the war, Pemberton was wounded in the Battle of Columbus. The Union attacked on Easter Sunday, April 16, 1865. Pemberton suffered both gunshot and sword wounds. Afterward, he tried to put the war behind him. He returned to his laboratory.

In the Lab

The year before the war began, Pemberton had founded J.S. Pemberton and Company of Columbus. His lab became known as the best in the country. He also helped run at least two drugstores.

At the time, drugstores often contained soda fountains. These popular meeting places offered syrups mixed with **carbonated** water. Some were medicines, while others were cool, sweet drinks. Doc Pemberton used soda fountains to test new flavors to see what customers liked.

In 1969, the Coca-Cola Company donated Pemberton's first home to the Historic Columbus Georgia Foundation. Today, the house is a museum honoring Pemberton.

In his lab, Pemberton mixed up potions used to relieve symptoms of illness. One, he called Globe Flower Cough Syrup. This big seller helped with lung problems. His Extract of Stillingia was used to treat ulcers and skin disorders. He also developed a popular perfume called Sweet Southern Bouquet. In addition, Pemberton made photography chemicals, hair dyes, and cosmetics at his lab.

In 1870, business brought the Pembertons to Atlanta, Georgia. The war-torn city was rebuilding. Pemberton seized a chance to create something new.

Pemberton's experience with chemistry and medicines would eventually lead to the invention of Coca-Cola.

Historic Recipe

Pemberton was a lifelong learner. In magazines, he read about new medical substances. Extracts of coca leaves and kola nuts were said to improve health. In 1885, he added them to a nerve tonic and headache cure he named French Wine Coca. He believed it was his best invention. In December, he formed the Pemberton Chemical Company. Three partners handled business and marketing.

Today, Pemberton's recipe is kept locked in the World of Coca-Cola in Atlanta, Georgia.

At the same time, the **temperance** movement was growing. Knowing this could hurt sales of his products, Pemberton began working on a new recipe that did not include wine. He wanted to be ready when Atlanta declared local **prohibition** in the summer of 1886.

Into a three-legged brass
kettle, Pemberton poured extracts
of kola nuts and coca leaves. Lime,
orange, vanilla, nutmeg, lemon,
and other secret oils added flavor. He
cooked his brew over a fire, stirring it with a
wooden paddle as big as an oar. He filtered the sauce and let it
ripen. Throughout the winter and spring of 1886, Pemberton sent his
mixture to Jacobs' **Pharmacy** in downtown Atlanta for taste testing.

Pemberton still thought of his syrup as a medicine. He called
it an "Intellectual Beverage and **Temperance** Drink." His business
partner Frank Robinson came up with a better idea. He named it
Coca-Cola after coca leaves and kola nuts. It used two Cs because
Robinson thought they looked nice for ads. The syrup had a great
flavor, a catchy name, and a nice logo. Coca-Cola was ready to sell.

Refreshing!

Jacobs' **Pharmacy** served the very first fountain Coca-Cola. On May 8, 1886, Coca-Cola went on sale there. An ounce of delicious caramel syrup was mixed with sparkling bubbly water. Customers could buy a glass of Coca-Cola at the soda fountain for five cents.

On May 29, Coca-Cola's first advertisement appeared in the *Atlanta Journal*. Coca-Cola was promoted as "Delicious! Refreshing! Exhilarating! Invigorating!" Soon, big banners hung over pharmacy doors. They read, "Drink Coca-Cola 5¢" so people knew the product was a new beverage they should try.

Pemberton insisted Coca-Cola was a medicine. His brain tonic relieved headaches. And he called

A Coca-Cola ad from the 1880s

it "my **temperance** drink." But for Robinson, it was a delicious soda! He wanted to focus on promoting it. But when **prohibition** ended in Atlanta in 1887, Pemberton returned his focus to French Wine Coca instead.

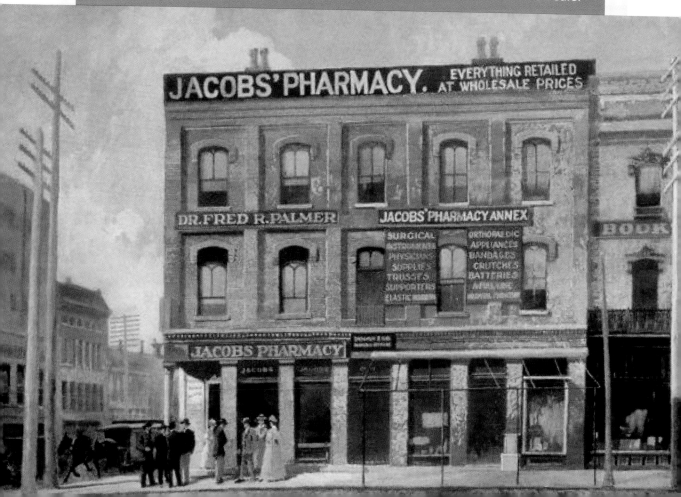

Druggist Willis Venable ran Jacobs' Pharmacy when Coca-Cola first went on sale.

An Inventor Gone

As Coca-Cola began to succeed, Pemberton formed the Coca-Cola Company. He received five cents for every gallon sold. He filed to incorporate the company on March 24, 1888. At the same time, Pemberton knew he was in very poor health. So, he prepared to sell the Coca-Cola recipe.

For a while, there was confusion over who owned the rights to both the Coca-Cola name and its recipe. The contract finally fell to one person.

Like Pemberton, Asa Griggs Candler was a **pharmacist** in Atlanta. He and his wife, Lucy Elizabeth Howard, had five children. Candler was eager for success. In the end, he gained the rights to Pemberton's secret recipe and the name for $2,300.

Pemberton died at home in Atlanta on August 16, 1888. He was buried in Linwood Cemetery in Columbus. On the day of his funeral, Atlanta pharmacists honored Pemberton. They closed their drugstores and attended the funeral service. For that one day, not a drop of Coca-Cola was served.

Asa Candler went on to serve as mayor of Atlanta from 1916 to 1919.

New Marketing

Candler worked hard to keep Coca-Cola going. In 1889, Candler sold 2,171 gallons (8,218 L) of syrup. That was enough for nearly 61,000 glasses of Coca-Cola!

Candler also used coupons to help promote Coca-Cola. This was long before coupons were as popular as they are today. He asked **pharmacists** for customers' names and then sent them coupons for one free drink. He gave the pharmacists twice as much syrup as they needed to honor the coupons.

A Coca-Cola ad from the 1890s

DRINK
DELICIOUS
Coca-Cola

Serving trays were one of the many ways Coca-Cola promoted its name.

If customers came back, the **pharmacy** would make money on the rest of the syrup. If they came back again and again, Coca-Cola would benefit, too.

On January 31, 1893, the **trademark** "Coca-Cola" was registered at the US **Patent** Office. Then in 1895, the drink was promoted as a soft drink instead of a medicine. That brought in more customers. Plus, gifts helped promote the product. Fans, lamps, toys, calendars, clocks, bookmarks, and other items carried the logo.

Sales soared. Coca-Cola factories opened in Texas, Illinois, Pennsylvania, and California. In 1890, the company sold 9,000 gallons (34,000 L) of syrup. By 1900, it sold more than 370,000 gallons (1.4 million L). Customers could find Coca-Cola in every US state and in Canada. The soda fountain business remained strong. But a new idea was taking Coca-Cola even further.

Bottling Business

In the back of a candy store in Vicksburg, Mississippi, was a small bottling operation. Its owner, Joseph Biedenharn, poured Coca-Cola into bottles beginning in 1894. He sold them to country people such as farmers and lumberers who were not near soda fountains.

Biedenharn's bottling idea came at the perfect time. When he began, glass had to be hand blown into molds. But before long, factories were mass-producing glass containers by machine. Factories then filled and sealed the bottles. When opened, they made a popping sound. That's how soda pop got its name!

Biedenharn had not asked permission to bottle Coca-Cola. Luckily, when he sent a case to the Coca-Cola Company, Candler said it was fine. But Candler wasn't very interested in bottling at the time. He believed soda fountains would continue to be people's main source for drinking Coca-Cola.

In 1899, Candler granted all US bottling rights to two Tennessee businessmen, Benjamin F. Thomas and Joseph P. Whitehead, for

When the Candler Building opened (center, seen in 1952), it was the tallest building in Atlanta. It remains an important property in the city today.

just one dollar! That year, Candler sold the first barrels of Coca-Cola syrup to bottling companies. He felt bottling was expensive. But, he also understood it would make Coca-Cola available to more people.

Between bottling and soda fountain sales, Coca-Cola's success continued and Candler became a millionaire. In 1906, he built the impressive Candler Building in Atlanta to house the Coca-Cola Company.

Competition

A timeline of Coca-Cola bottles

In 1906, the US Congress created the Pure Food and Drug Act. Under the new law, companies had to label food products truthfully and avoid harmful ingredients. This actually helped Coca-Cola. Many other companies had created products with names that sounded like "Coca-Cola." Now, the real thing would be known by its name and its safe ingredients.

Still, the government thought Coca-Cola contained too much **caffeine**. In 1909, it seized 40 barrels and 20 kegs of syrup. In the end, Coca-Cola reduced the soda's caffeine content by half.

Coca-Cola always had competition. Colas were common! To make Coca-Cola **unique**, the company wanted a new bottle. An employee of the Root Glass Company in Terre Haute, Indiana, drew the design. Earl Dean based the shape on a cacao bean, which is where chocolate comes from. He didn't know what a kola nut looked like!

In 1916, the design was approved at the Coca-Cola Bottlers Convention. The logo was part of the bottle, rather than on a paper label. Best of all, the curvy shape was easy to recognize, even in the dark! Now, no one could mistake another cola for the real thing.

The bottle became an important symbol of Coca-Cola. The shape became a registered trademark in 1977.

The Cola Wars

In 1916, Asa Candler stepped down. In 1919, Coca-Cola sold for $25 million to Robert Woodruff. Sales dropped. In 1918, the company had sold 18.7 million gallons (70.8 million L) of syrup. But in 1922, it sold just 15.4 million gallons (58.3 million L).

Robert's son Ernest took over in 1923 and would lead the company for decades. While he was in charge, many important ideas were introduced. This included the six-pack carton. Also, metal coolers were made to keep Coca-Cola ice-cold. Now, customers could easily carry the soda home. In addition, red became the Coca-Cola color. Even delivery trucks had to be red.

Coca-Cola and Pepsi-Cola are still seen as major competitors in the beverage industry.

Coca-Cola grew. Bottling plants opened in Europe, South America, and Africa. The logo appeared in Spanish bullfighting arenas and on Canadian sled dog teams. Coca-Cola followed the US Olympic team to the Netherlands in 1928. That year, for the first time, more Coca-Cola sold in bottles than at soda fountains.

Coca-Cola still cost just five cents for a six and a half ounce bottle. No other soda could compete until the mid 1930s. Suddenly, Pepsi-Cola offered 12 ounces for the same price. For decades, the two companies competed neck and neck in the "cola wars." They held the number one and number two places in the soda industry.

From 1928 to 1935, famous American artist Norman Rockwell made six paintings that helped advertise Coca-Cola.

Cultural Symbol

By the start of **World War II**, Coca-Cola was in 44 countries. During the war, factories supplied US troops with Coca-Cola. In 1945, the year the war ended, the familiar shortened name "Coke" became a registered **trademark**.

In time, the company expanded its product list. It purchased the rights to Fanta in 1946 and introduced Sprite in 1961. The company purchased Minute Maid in 1960. Its first diet cola, Tab, arrived in 1963. And in 1966, Fresca became part of the Coca-Cola brand.

Coca-Cola had grown so big that it was a **cultural** symbol. In the 1970s, the company came up with a song for a new television commercial. It gained instant attention and seemed to capture people's hearts. Called the "Hilltop" commercial, the song featured Coke's **slogan**, "It's the Real Thing."

At the same time, Roberto Goizueta was working his way up in the company. He was born in Cuba in 1931. There, he started out as a chemical engineer at a Coca-Cola bottling plant. He moved to the United States in 1960. In 1981, he became CEO of the company.

Coca-Cola president Donald Keough (left) and CEO
Roberto Goizueta (right) toast to New Coke in 1985.

Under Goizueta, the company continued to prosper. In 1982, it introduced Diet Coke. On July 12, 1985, Coke even went into space! Astronauts aboard the space shuttle *Challenger* tested the Coca-Cola Space Can. The same year, Coke had a misstep. It changed its recipe. Customers hated New Coke! So, Coca-Cola Classic soon returned.

The Real Thing

Today, Coca-Cola is the world's largest beverage company and Coke is the best-known soft drink. The company's global headquarters is still in Atlanta. Doc Pemberton's recipe is still top secret. Coca-Cola has a simple principle. For a small price, customers get a moment of refreshment. But, it happens more than 1 billion times a day!

The company now owns many brands. Sprite, Dr. Pepper, Fanta, Minute Maid, and Dasani are all on the list. Coke is sold in more than 200 countries. Worldwide, the company employs more than 700,000 people.

Many events led to Coca-Cola's historic success. But, it all began with a medical recipe. Dr. John Pemberton created the Coca-Cola taste. With hard work, he contributed greatly to the field of medicine. He never imagined the enormous success of his "brain tonic."

The Coca-Cola Company has not forgotten him. A statue of Doc Pemberton stands outside the World of Coca-Cola, located at Pemberton Place in Atlanta. It honors the efforts of a popular **pharmacist** who made Coca-Cola possible.

Today, Coca-Cola runs more than 900 plants around the world. The word "Coca-Cola" is recognized by more people than any other word except "okay."

Timeline

1831 John Stith Pemberton was born on January 8 in Georgia.

1850 Pemberton graduated from Reform Medical College in Macon, Georgia.

1853 Pemberton married Ann Eliza Clifford "Cliff" Lewis.

1854 Pemberton's son, Charles Ney, was born.

1860 Pemberton founded J.S. Pemberton and Company of Columbus.

1865 Pemberton was wounded in the Battle of Columbus.

1870 The Pembertons moved to Atlanta, Georgia.

1885 Pemberton formed the Pemberton Chemical Company.

1886 The Coca-Cola recipe was completed; Coca-Cola went on sale at Jacobs' Pharmacy in Atlanta, Georgia, for five cents a glass.

1888 On March 24, Pemberton filed to incorporate the Coca-Cola Company; John Pemberton died in Atlanta on August 16.

Catchphrases

In every decade, Coca-Cola has come up with catchy slogans.

1886 – Drink Coca-Cola

1904 – Delicious and Refreshing

1917 – Three Million a Day

1929 – The Pause that Refreshes

1932 – Ice Cold Sunshine

1938 – The Best Friend Thirst Ever Had

1948 – Where There's Coke There's Hospitality

1958 – The Cold, Crisp Taste of Coke

1969 – It's the Real Thing

1979 – Have a Coke and Smile

1982 – Coke Is It!

1993 – Always Coca-Cola

2009 – Open Happiness

Glossary

caffeine - a substance that makes you feel more awake. It is found in coffee, tea, and other products.

carbonated - combined or infused with carbon dioxide.

chemistry - a science that focuses on substances and the changes they go through.

civil war - a war between groups in the same country. The United States of America and the Confederate States of America fought a civil war from 1861 to 1865.

culture - the customs, arts, and tools of a nation or a people at a certain time. Something related to culture is cultural.

enlist - to join the armed forces voluntarily.

patent - the exclusive right granted to a person to make or sell an invention. This right lasts for a certain period of time.

pharmacy - a store in which drugs are made and sold. A pharmacist is a person licensed to prepare and sell drugs.

prohibition - the banning of the sale and production of alcoholic beverages.

slogan - a word or a phrase used to express a position, a stand, or a goal.

stagecoach - a horse-drawn coach used to carry people and goods from place to place.

temperance - relating to a social movement that urged people to avoid drinking alcoholic beverages.

trademark - something such as a word that identifies a certain company. It cannot be used by others without permission.

unique (yoo-NEEK) - being the only one of its kind.

World War II - from 1939 to 1945, fought in Europe, Asia, and Africa.

Websites

To learn more about Food Dudes,
visit **booklinks.abdopublishing.com**. These links are routinely monitored and updated to provide the most current information available.

Index